Passive Income

Definitive Beginner's Guide to Quit Your Day Job Through Multiple Income Streams

Table of Contents

Introduction

Congratulations on purchasing *Passive Income: Definitive Beginner's Guide to Quit Your Day Job Through Multiple Income Streams* and thank you for doing so. Earning a passive income is a great way to move away from the grind of the traditional 9 to 5 job, but finding the right one for you and sticking with it can be more difficult than it might first appear.

To wit, the following chapters will discuss everything you need to know about successfully starting a passive income stream and seeing it through to financial security. You will also learn the best ways to perform online retail arbitrage either by using Amazon and eBay in combination or by simply signing up to be a Fulfillment by Amazon Seller. From there you will find a discussion on the many ways to create digital content and sell it for a profit be it webinars, eBooks or stock photos. Finally, you will learn about using real estate to generate passive income either by investing in real estate property, investing in REITs or purchasing contracts for properties with potential and then wholesaling them for a profit.

While some people out there will naturally stick their noses up at what they perceive to be just another get rich quick scheme, the reality is that passive income is a secret that many of the richest, and most famous people in the world use to maintain their bank accounts while to all appearances they are simply living the good life. In fact, studies show that out of all of the millionaires in America, more than 60 percent have at least three streams of income, while nearly 50 percent have four or more and over 30 percent have five or more.

For example, movie icon Ashton Kutcher understands the importance of passive income which is why he invests in technology companies. In 2009, Kutcher jumped on the Skype bandwagon early and got in for $2.75 per share. Microsoft has since purchased Skype for a price in excess of $8 billion. Along similar lines, while he may not have been great at managing California's budget, former governor Arnold Schwarzenegger is savvy enough with his own money that a majority of his income these days comes from profitable real estate investments that he made with money he earned from bodybuilding competitions before he even started acting. Finally, business icon Warren Buffet currently has 15 different passive income streams making him money 24/7.

There are plenty of books on this subject on the market, thanks again for choosing this one! Every effort was made to ensure it is full of as much useful information as possible, please enjoy!

Chapter 1:
Passive Income-
What You Need to Know

As the job market migrates towards more and more of a temporary arrangement type of situation, it can be hard to believe that not so very long ago a person could expect to work for a single company for 40 or even 50 years and then retire, secure in the fact that the company they gave their life to would, in turn, take care of them. As company pensions are quickly becoming extinct, this means those who are part of the work force today need to be ready and able to take care of themselves if they ever hope to retire.

Unfortunately, current estimates suggest that in order to retire successfully, the retiree needs to have about $500,000 banked if they want to continue on in the fashion to which they have become accustomed. Simply put, the best way to ensure that you have the money you need, when it comes time for you to need it, is to start looking into passive income options as soon as possible. Passive income streams are ways of making money that continue paying out even after you stop actively focusing on them. While many passive income entrepreneurs have gone fully digital, there is still some income to be made in the real world as well, which is why subsequent chapters will cover ways to generate a passive income in the digital, as well as the physical, world.

While saving for the future is an admirable goal, passive income is also the best choice for anyone who feels as though they can currently be earning more money, while doing less work. While these days many people have accepted the 40-hour work week as a way of life until they die, in reality, active income simply isn't enough for many people to cover their bills, let alone generate a level of wealth that actually leaves them comfortable. If this sounds like you, then the sooner you start multitasking your income streams, the better.

While setting up an income stream will require you to put in extra hours up front, with very little (if any) compensation, the amount that it ultimately brings in over time will more than make up for the amount of unpaid effort that goes into setting it up. Even better, once you have 4 or 5 different passive streams set up you will one day find that you don't even need to worry about your day job anymore. Utilizing passive income streams will never mean that you are free from any and all work, it will mean that you will have to work much less on average than a person who makes as much as you do but generates it via active income.

Even better, in these increasingly uncertain economic times, knowing that you always have some passive income coming in can grant you the true security that comes from knowing you are financially sound no matter what comes. While you may not be able to say goodbye to your current job right away, you will soon be amazed at how much less of a headache it is once you don't have to worry about it as your sole source of income. What's more, having your passive income backing you up might just be the push you need to get out there and find an active income stream you actually enjoy as well. Regardless of what it leads to, there is no doubt about it, have a passive income stream up and running is the first step to being the arbiter of your financial destiny.

What you need to get started creating passive income opportunities

While there are obviously benefits that come along with having a traditional high paying 9 to 5 job, there are never going to be more than 24 hours in a given day which means there will always be an ultimate limit to your earning potential. This is the heart of why so many people find passive income so attractive, it lets them determine how much money they want to make on their schedule, not based on what a timesheet says. To ensure you get off on the right foot, however, consider the following requirements first.

1. *Make sure you have the time:* Despite the fact that they will eventually require very little time in return for a realistic payout, if you hope to get a passive income stream up and running without putting in the leg work for doing so, you are going to be sadly disappointed. Even if you ultimately plan on having someone else do the majority of the actual work when it comes to getting the stream up and running, you are still going to need to do the required research to ensure that you are making the most of the type of passive income stream you ultimately do end up investing in. In fact, possibly the biggest determining factor as to the future success that your budding passive income stream generates is the amount of research you put in to ensure it gets up and running successfully at the beginning.

2. *Patience:* When getting started with a new passive income stream, it is important to approach it with realistic expectations as to how long you may realistically be putting work into the project without seeing any real results. Even those passive income streams that can be set up relatively quickly will still

7

take at least a month or two to start generating any income at all, and it likely won't be all that much at first. Understanding what to expect is crucial to prevent yourself from giving up hope and quitting before you get to the actually payoff of the passive income stream you are working on. Even if you expect the passive income stream to never amount to anything major, it is important to always stick with it until it is actually producing. Remember, a little passive income is always going to be more profitable than no passive income at all.

3. *The right mental state:* While at first it might be hard to wrap your head around the idea that you can make money 24 hours a day, 365 days a year, it is important that you come around to the idea, not just as a neat theory, but as an indelible practice. This can be easier said than done, however, as modern society has likely trained you to view success as something that only comes after years and years of back breaking work. This means that if you want to commit yourself fully to the practice, you are going to have to work to actively cultivate the type of mindset that believes having a successful passive income stream is not only something that is possible, it is something that is in reach right now.

If you find yourself having trouble getting into the passive income mindset, you might find it effective to start by having an honest and open conversation with yourself about your goals for the future and how passive income can help you meet them. You may find that by taking the potential passive income stream out of the realm of a pie in the sky possibility and plugging it into your actual plan for the future it becomes easier to truly accept as a realistic possibility.

From there you can then consider the types of passive income streams that could be the most effective for you based on your passions and proclivities. Choosing a passive income stream that you truly feel passionate about is another great way to get past any mental roadblocks you might have as to its overall success. This doesn't mean that you should blindly commit to the first passive income strategy you come across, as you should still be on the lookout for realistic flaws in any plan, it just means you shouldn't let societal prejudices get in the way of your potential success.

4. *A clear plan:* After you have ultimately decided on the type of passive income stream that you are interested in pursuing, the first thing you are going to want to do in order to ensure you get started on achieving your goal on the right foot is to determine exactly what steps you need to take to ensure the type of success that you are looking for. It is important to have a clear idea of what the various to steps are going to be as well as all of the sub goals that you are going to need to reach to ensure your end goal is successful. Not only will this help you further ensure the likelihood of your success, it will help you understand just what you are in for if you hope to see the passive income stream through to the finish line.

Outside of just letting you know what it is you are getting into, having a clear plan will help you to move more quickly from one task to the next without getting bogged down in wondering what you need to do and when. If you proceed without having a precise plan it will make it much easier for you to remain idle if things get difficult, thus decreasing your chance of ever actually seeing the results of all of your hard work.

5. *A clear timetable:* In addition to having a clear plan for what you need to do in order to get your passive income stream off of the ground, you are also going to want to know roughly how long each of the steps should take. Additionally, you will find that having a clear end goal as well as a firm idea of how long it will take you to get there will make it much easier to get the steps in between done much more quickly. The goal here is to ensure that you remain motivated throughout the process, and always having a looming deadline is a great place to start.

6. *Dedication to the task at hand:* While you are working to set up your first passive income stream, especially if you are doing so on the cheap and by yourself, you will likely come across at least one point where you will begin to doubt that what you are doing is really possible. During these periods it is important that you remember what it is that you are going through all of this trouble for and how much easier things will be once the passive income stream is up and functioning on all cylinders. Remember, everyone faces obstacles when it comes to reaching their goals, what separates those who are perpetually successful from those who perpetually aren't is their ability to persevere when the going gets tough.

Chapter 2:
All About Arbitrage

While you might not be familiar with the word arbitrage, odds are you are familiar with its core concepts. Essentially, it is buying a commodity or a specific product at a low price and then selling it for a higher price to someone else. While the term originally applied to currency markets, the rise of the internet has made retail arbitrage, not only possible, but often one of the cheapest and easiest ways to set up your own passive income stream. No matter what type you choose to pursue, this passive income stream will see you shopping around for the cheapest items and then reselling at an existing price point to ensure that you always make a profit.

Getting started

The first thing you are going to need in order to ever make any money at online retail arbitrage is a good nose for finding a bargain; baring that, however, there are a few applications that can help you compensate. The first two are for Amazon and eBay respectively, and they will allow you to scan an item's barcode to determine what the product is selling for in real time on the service in question. Simply search for Amazon Price check and eBay application in your app store of choice and you will find what you need to get started right away. This will let you know what the baseline price for the item you are considering currently is which means you will never have to take a risk on a product that you purchase.

Besides the free applications, the first expense for this passive income stream is going to come from an application known as Profit Bandit. It costs $10 up front, but for this investment you get access to wealth of data that includes how the current price of an item stacks up with its average in the recent past. It will also let you know if you will be competing with Amazon directly on the item that you are selling or if it is against Amazon's code of conduct to sell it for some reason. Finally, it even automatically calculates out how much profit you are going to make based on the price you have found, the price the item is selling for and even factors in shipping.

Finding profitable items

When first learning about arbitrage, the minds of most people automatically go straight to big ticket items that would naturally include a hefty profit for the seller as well. While these items do appear occasionally, the reality is that you will earn a much greater and more reliable return selling common items that everyone needs eventually, than you will holding out for items that will help you to strike it rich. This advice isn't exciting, but it is sound and you will find that finding a sale on diapers or ink cartridges once could keep your arbitrage business profitable for quite some time.

Additional items you will want to consider include anything that is on sale or discounted, especially seasonal items that can be picked up for pennies on the dollar after the holiday has passed. As long as you are willing to hold onto them for nearly a year, you will find that these sorts of things never depreciate in value and can lead to large profit margins if you buy them at the right time. Once you stock up on holiday items you can then wait 9 months or so and get in on the early bird holiday market and make a reasonable return with very little risk. Alternatively, you can wait to just a few weeks before the holiday and post the items for even more money in hopes that you can take advantage of someone else's propensity for last minute shopping. The downside here is, of course, if the item doesn't sell then you are going to have to hold onto it for a whole extra year. You can also find success if you keep up with the latest trends and get in on certain items before their prices have increased to take advantage of newfound popularity.

Besides just looking for a good deal, it is important to think about how a certain item is going to ship before purchasing it, as you want to avoid lots of returns from items that are fragile. Likewise, you are going to want to ensure shipping costs are reasonable and that you aren't going to have to worry about complicated packaging or shipping regulations. Finally, if you are looking to get into online arbitrage for absolutely no money down, you will be surprised what items you can find around your house that others will actually be willing to pay for.

As a general rule, if you want to ensure that the products you are buying are going to be worth your time and effort you are going to want to stick to items that you can sell for at least 50 percent more than what you paid for them. The only exception to this is if you have a very specific plan in mind for the item at the time of purchase. When you are working out the potential for profit on various items, it is important to factor shipping into the equation as well, when applicable.

Chapter 3:
Fulfillment by Amazon

When it comes to putting as little time and effort into the online retail arbitrage as possible, the Fulfillment by Amazon program is a great place to start. FBA allows sellers to sell virtually any item under the sun, while offloading most of the work to Amazon itself. As such, sellers find items they want to sell before sending them to Amazon, who then takes care of the rest of the process including shipping the item, storing it before it sells and dealing with customers if something goes wrong. You just have to find the items, post them to Amazon.com and wait for a check in the mail every two weeks (the first check can take up to a month to arrive). The amount of each check will reflect the number of items you sold during a specific period, minus Amazon's cut, plus the fees for shipping and storage.

While not having to deal with the myriad of logistical issues that comes along with storage and shipping, not to mention customer service, is likely enough all by itself to warrant interest from many individuals interested in passive income, being a member of FBA also has other benefits as well. First and foremost, among these is the fact that items that are sold by FBA members are eligible for the free two-day shipping that Amazon Prime members are entitled too which means that your items are naturally going to be preferred over many competitors, even if it costs slightly more up front. This is because an Amazon Prime account costs a yearly fee of $150 which means that every Prime member is looking to amortize these costs over as many transactions as possible.

Maximizing your FBA account

In addition to the fees that you will pay for shipping and storage, and on top of their cut of each sale, Amazon also requires all FBA sellers pay a $40 monthly fee as well. This means that if you are hoping to do more than pay Amazon $40 a month, you are going to want to do as much as you can to ensure the cost is worthwhile. The first thing you are going to want to do is download the Amazon's Seller Application which will allow you to see what you stand to make on a given item at a price you select after all relevant FBA fees have been accounted for. This is crucial to maximizing your profits and cannot be recommended highly enough.

Additionally, the seller app will also give you a precise account of the number of other individuals who are currently trying to sell the same item, while also showing you which brands are the most popular in certain categories. To take this type of research a step further, you are going to want to seek out a purchasing statistics website such as CamelCamelCamel.com. These websites allow you to take the Amazon.com based URL that you provide and show you the pricing and popularity of similar items over a specific period of time. They are also extremely important to ensure that not only are you selling the item for a price that you can take advantage of, but you are getting the best price for the item possible in the grand scheme of things as well.

FBA Success Tips

- *Consider Niche Products:* If you are familiar with a specific niche and understand the wants and needs of the audience in question, then this can easily be an easy FBA money maker assuming a few things hold true.

First, you are going to want to ensure that there is enough of a demand for the products you are considering, while at the same time not so much demand that you have trouble beating out the competition. Assuming the types of products that you have in mind meet these qualifications then the next thing you are going to want to determine is if you can find the items in question for a price that is cheap enough to ensure you actually make a profit.

- *Consider each purchase carefully:* The best online retail arbitrage products are those that are heavily discounted, irrespective of the type of product in question. As a general rule, if you find anything, literally anything that is marked down 75 percent from its original price, then you can likely find a way to sell it for a profit online; whether it is worth it is another question. Another great choice are items that you can purchase in bulk cheaply now, before waiting for natural scarcity to set in six months or so down the line when your investment will pay off in spades.

A great example of this are toys you can purchase from a dollar store that are based on properties that are never going to go out of style such as Disney properties like Princesses, Star Wars or Marvel superheroes. Many of these products are only ever sold at dollar stores which means that after the initial stock dries up there will be thousands of parents out there looking for character specific merchandise that their child has not consumed yet. If you aren't interested in waiting, you can instead group a number of themed items together, knock a fraction of the total profit off and sell the total as a true bargain.

For example, if you purchase five Disney Princess puzzles for a total of $5, knowing that each typically sells for $5 on Amazon, then you can sell all five for $20, still have the group seen as the value, and even make more than a 50 percent profit on the transaction. If you pursue this course of action, you are going to generate a unique UPC code for the group of products, though you can use the same UPC code for multiple groups if applicable.

- *Never stop looking for the best deals:* While places like dollar stores or bulk discount big box retailers are occasionally going to have major sales that you can profit from, in the long run you are always going to find the best in less obvious locations. The best place to start is with local business as you never know when you might be able to take advantage of a local merchant's connections, and lack of an online store, to make a profit. All of their items aren't going to be cheaper than other options, but now and then you can find common items dramatically underpriced compared to the competition. It is important to treat these types of finds like a renewable resource and only buy a certain amount at a time to ensure the business doesn't get suspicious and raise the price in response to increased demand.

- *Be aware of your seller rating:* When you are first looking for items to stock on your FBA page, it can be tempting to go after the absolutely cheapest items you can find, regardless of quality, this is folly however, as doing so will start you out with a middling rating which will hurt your overall profit potential in the long term. Especially early on, Amazon will also actually be monitoring your rating to ensure you are not hurting the FBA brand by dealing in shoddy items, keep everything on the up and up and Amazon, as well as your customers, will walk away happy.

Chapter 4:
Online Retail Arbitrage Via eBay

If you like the idea of buying items and then selling them online for a profit, but aren't interested in actually going out and purchasing physical items, then online retail arbitrage via eBay might be more your style. While traditional FBA arbitrage involves periods of work finding items and then stretches where passive income is generated off of that work, eBay arbitrage uses Amazon for a low level amount of work for each bundle of related sales generated.

Specifically, in this instance you take the time to keep tabs of the overall pricing patterns of numerous common items on Amazon, while at the same time keeping track of the price for those same items on eBay. Once you find a disparity between the two that is big enough to be worth your while, you then list the item on eBay, purchase the item on Amazon and then send the item to the actual buyer. While Amazon isn't a fan, you can also list the item before buying it and then simply gift it to the seller once it has been purchased. Maximize your potential for profit in this scenario by following the steps outlined below.

1. *Choose the right items:* When dealing with eBay online retail arbitrage the trick lies in not only finding the right price in the moment, but finding the right price that is going to stick around long enough for you to post your item now and to still make a profit. What's more, unlike on Amazon where the prices are likely to remain relatively stable, if you back the wrong item on eBay the baseline price can easily change several times over the course of a single day. As such, instead of playing the field as a whole, it is better to choose a niche of items, so that you can learn when certain prices swing in a

profitable direction. Again, the best choice is to stick with something you know, barring electronics because you will never be able to lowball dealers from overseas.

2. *List items thoughtfully:* Once you find an item that you know you can make a profit on, the next thing you are going to want to do is list it on eBay in a way that it attracts as many potential buyers as possible. First and foremost, this means never posting multiples of the same item at the same time as doing so makes it appear to potential bidders as though there is a surplus of the item which means they are going to be less anxious to bid as eagerly as they might otherwise be if there were only a single copy of the item in question. Additionally, only posting a single item at a time will prevent you from losing money if the price drops out of the item you are selling and forces you to commit to an unprofitable transaction.

3. *List items properly:* When you do decide to list a single item, it is important that you take the time to include as much details about the item as possible as well as multiple quality photos. Ideally you will want a picture of the product in use, as well as a scale picture of the product in question to ensure that the buyer doesn't feel cheated once they receive the item. When filling out the listing it is important to try and come up with a catchy title, and use the description to make the product sound like both a good deal and one that is not likely to come along again anytime soon. You are also going to want to include specific details, though nothing that will make it easier for the buyer to look the item up on Amazon and spoil your plan entirely.

4. *Ensure you actually pull the trigger:* Finally, it is important that you do not actually get so caught up in playing the disparity between the services against one another that you perpetually hold off from actually posting any items yourself. Remember, it doesn't matter that you always get the best price for items, it matters that you sell items quickly and reliable to maximize the amount of time your passive income investment funds can actually be out in the field and generating a tangible return.

Chapter 5:
Creating Your Own Webinar

While investing in FBA or eBay online retail arbitrage is certainly profitable, if the idea of always finding new things to sell seems cumbersome, then selling digital products might be a better choice for you. Creating digital content takes much more time, or possibly income, up front, but after the original content has been created and starts generating a profit, the amount of additional effort you put into the endeavor is entirely up to you. This after the fact effort is largely going to be in the marketing department, which again can be outsourced if you feel the need.

If you are interested in creating your own webinar, the first thing you are going to need to ask yourself is what talents, skills, hobbies or interests that you have that you have mastered to the point where other people will consider you an expert on the topic at hand. Remember, you need to not only be fluent in the skill you are planning to outline, but also will need to have a clear idea of how best to teach others to replicate what you have learned. Additionally, it is important to keep in mind the type of information that people are willing to pay for is typically going to need to be either high level, or packaged with a spin that makes potential customers think that buying your webinar is a better choice than using the free YouTube alternative. If you aren't sure if you have this type of skill, consider the following.

1. *Start by listing off all of your strengths:* While many people start off interested in creating a webinar, they often leave disappointed that they don't have anything to teach, not because this is actually true, but because they limit themselves in terms of what they consider

something that can be taught. The first thing that comes to mind for many people are obvious skills relating to things like business or personal fitness. When making a list of suitable topics, you need to expand your definition, however, and instead consider what you may well think of as innate qualities things like organizational or time management skills. If you are so good at something that you don't think it even warrants notice, you might want to consider it for this purpose.

2. *Consider how to express the content as clearly as possible:* The best approach as to how you are going to shoot your webinar is going to depend almost entirely on the type of content that you are dealing with. In some instances, you will find that a basic lecture with relevant explanatory pictures or a narrated PowerPoint presentation might be enough while other times a narrated video might be the best choice. The exact way you go about spreading the information doesn't matter nearly as much as the fact that you have a professional sounding audio stream to go along with the visuals that you provide. Even if this means you need to factor in expenses for a professional sounding microphone, you need to do whatever is necessary to ensure that you make the right sort of impression early on or your initial viewers will end up being your only viewers.

3. *Hosting your content:* If you plan on making a single webinar, then you should start off on the right foot by planning to host several more to take advantage of the popularity of the first. This means you are good to need to create and host your own website so you have a place that people can go to in order to actually view your content. If you have never made a website before then you will be happy to know that the process has been

dramatically streamlined over the years. This means that typing "website free trial" is all you really need to do in order to see many of the most popular website building tools on the market today.

These starter services will allow you to create a basic website that will more than meet your needs through a simple and well curated process. While many of the most popular platforms can be accessed for free, you will want to invest enough in the website so that you have your own unique domain name. Having an official web address will naturally make your webinar seem more legitimate which will, in turn, make visitors more likely to actually pay for it.

4. *Fill out your website:* When it comes to filling up the online space that you have purchased, you are going to want to include more than just a simple PayPal buy now button and a few details about your webinar. Rather, you are going to want to do everything in your power to ensure that you get as many people through the door as possible by making it clear to them that you actually know whatever it is that you are trying to teach them. A good way to get started down this path is to write up a number of blog posts that all deal with basic aspects of the topic you are charging people to learn about. You can even include other videos that show you being good at the thing you are talking about. All of the content that you create should then point your potential customers towards your webinar if they are interested in learning more.

5. *Market yourself the right way:* While this step is technically optional, it is highly encouraged as it will increase the effectiveness of this type of passive income

stream nearly every time. When it comes to getting the word out about your webinar, the first thing you are going to want to do is to spread the word via social media and ask everyone you know to do the same; you never know when something might go viral, and a good webinar can bounce around via word of mouth for quite some time. You can even offer a discount to those who spread the word via social media. From there, the next place you are going to want to go it so anywhere that people who might be interested in your webinar might congregate online. These types of spaces typically have message boards filled with questions from clueless individuals who are just looking for a little information. Answer lots of questions and crediting the answers to your website can go a long way towards building a target audience. Finally, you are going to want to consider your SEO as well, and don't be afraid to pay someone to optimize it for you if you don't know how to do it yourself.

From there you will want to seek out various blogs on related to the general field that your webinar falls into and reach out to the writers of those blogs and see if you can contribute guest content. Every blog post that you write that is filled with the right type of high quality and relevant content is a great advertisement for your webinar. In addition to including a link to your site in every post, this will help to get your name out among the community that you are targeting. Over time, your goal should be to be seen as an absolute expert on the topic in question and there is no better way of doing so than ensuring that your name is said in the same breath as your topic as possible.

6. *Develop an email list:* Once you manage to start getting paying customers, the most important thing you can do in order to ensure that the passive income stream that you are developing really has legs to it is to ask individuals if they are interested in signing up for your email newsletter while they are purchasing your product. This way, if you decide to release another product, you already know a bunch of individuals who might be interested in in purchasing it. If you go on to follow the steps below when it comes to creating your own eBook, then giving it away for free is a great to get additional email newsletter subscribers as well.

   Once you have started successfully getting new email subscribers, you are going to want to ensure that you are producing content that for them to read. The rate at which you put out new email newsletters is up to you, though a good rule of thumb is to do so often enough that your readers, especially those who are paying customers, don't forget about you, which will make it easier to convince them to buy your new product when the time is right. When it comes to content you are going to want to always include a 90/10 split where 90 percent of the content is relevant based on the topic of your webinar and 10 percent is an advertisement for your products.

The content that you create for your email blast is a great way to further convince people that you are an expert in your field, and creating new content will ensure that your newsletter open rates remain high. As long as you continue creating unique, worthwhile content that presents a persona that is one with the community in question, then you can expect your email newsletter email list to continue growing and when it comes time to sell new content you will see it begin to bear fruit.

Chapter 6:
Write an eBook

If you are knowledgeable on a given topic but don't want to have to go to all of the trouble of recording something or building your own website, then writing an eBook on the topic might be the solution you were looking for. Additionally, if you don't want to write the book in question, then there are numerous websites such as UpWork.com where you can hire a freelancer to do it for you. Once you have the content of the book you can then pay a small fee to have someone format it and create a cover, or you can do so yourself with free programs readily available online.

With an eBook in hand, you can then post it, for free, to Amazon's Kindle Marketplace where you will then make a percentage of the total profits of each sale with the rest going back to Amazon. If you go this route, you can expect Amazon to take 70 percent of the profits of books priced below $2.99 and above $9.99 and only 35 percent for books between $2.99 and $9.99. This means that you will want to price your books between $2.99 and $9.99 in order to make the maximum profit possible. The most common books on the market today are those in the how to or self-help genres and people are always looking or new takes on old problems. That's why eBooks have been outselling traditional books since the early 2010s.

Decide what to write about: When it comes to finding the right topic to write about, if you made a webinar, then the best place to start is with that same information, but simply packaged in a different form. If you are starting from scratch, or looking to have someone write something for you, then you should instead focus on a topic that can be researched readily, while still remaining arcane enough to prevent people from just going out and doing the research themselves. Furthermore, once you do find a topic that you think is promising you are going to want to visit the Kindle Marketplace and ensure that your particular take on the topic in question isn't already played out. It doesn't matter if the general topic has been covered, in order to find success, you are going to need to find something that you can put a unique spin on.

With a topic in mind, you are also going to want to consider who the target audience of your book is going to be. A book that is written for experts is very different than one that is written for beginners and having a clear idea of who you are writing for will make narrowing the topic down effectively much easier. Not only that, but writing with a target audience in mind will also make it easier for you to get nothing but 5 star reviews, the surest way to guarantee that the book you have written will be more than just a flash in the pan like many once popular eBooks.

Pay for a quality cover: While it might seem silly, in reality, and much as it has always been, nearly 90 percent of all eBook purchasing decisions are made based on the quality of the cover of the book in question. As such, it is important that you have the sort of cover that not only attracts attention, but presents you in an authoritative and professional fashion. You will also want to include a back cover that contains a catchy description that highlights the most important information that readers will find inside. Finally, if you have credentials that make your book seem authoritative, then you are going to want to ensure that they are prominently featured on the cover as well. This doesn't mean that you should ever consider faking credentials, however, as a quick online search is then all that is required to fill your reviews with 1 star ratings.

Chapter 7:
Sell Stock Photos Online

If you are already familiar with the basics as far as what makes a good picture and you already have a camera that is capable of taking high quality photos, then taking photographs for the express purpose of selling them to stock photo sites might be a viable way to easily create a new passive income stream. There are numerous different sites that you might be interested in, including the major players ShutterStock.com and iStockPhot.com and each allows photographers to post content to their website in return for a cut of the profits if a third party decides to license the use of the content in question for a project they are working on. Websites will typically take anywhere from 50 to 85 percent of the profits based on numerous different variables including things like the number of pictures that you have posted and your experience with previous professional photography. Regardless, however, selling stock photos is always going to be a numbers game which means you are going to want to stick with the following steps if you want your photos to be as profitable as possible.

1. *Know what type of pictures sell:* The first step to making a profit when selling photos online is not only knowing what types of pictures sell, but also how to reproduce the quality that is inherent in them as well. Assuming you already know a few things about taking a quality photograph, this means you are going to want to spend some time looking through the photographs that are on display in various categories that you think you might be interested in taking photographs in. Your goal should be to find a category that the site you are interested in applying for offers that has enough

pictures to indicate that there is a section of the audience that is interested in them, without being so crowded that it is unlikely that you will see a lot of hits, especially as a new photographer.

2. *Start taking pictures:* Once you have a clear idea of the types of picture that you are interested in taking, you are going to want to get out there and start taking pictures. You are going to want to use something nicer than your phone as well, you don't need to break the bank, but the camera you use should be indicative of the quality of the pictures you hope to take. You are going to want to start by taking practice shots of the subjects that you plan on submitting to the stock photo sites so that you get a good feel for what qualities make for the best shots in that genre.

   After you have a number of shots that you feel as though are good enough to submit to the site of your choice, you are going to want to blow the up to the largest possible size and take a long hard look at each to ensure that they are as close to perfect as you can make them. You never know what size of picture your potential client is looking for which means not looking at your pictures at the maximum size is akin to gambling with your potential profits. Aside from that, remember to always stick with an exposure rate of 100 percent and to use a tripod as often as possible as blurry pictures are rarely going to be accepted until it is done for effect.

3. *Submit your photos:* First you are going to need to submit your photos to the site of your choice, and then once they have been accepted you will need to create your own profile. Once you are given free rein to post

new pictures as you will, you will then want to upload each photo with descriptive text regarding what is in the picture as well as a host of descriptive keywords that will help to ensure your photos show up in as many different relevant searches as possible. While you will want to include outside of the box keyword ideas, you don't want to go so far as listing your photos using inaccurate keywords. While this will help your photos to get in front of as many different pairs of eyes as possible, it won't actually help them to be seen. Remember, if your photos are everywhere all of the time people will start to automatically tune them out.

4. *Promote your photos properly:* A majority of the most frequently used stock photo websites offer up free sections where photographers can add photos if they so choose that are available for limited use free of charge. While at first blush it may seem counterintuitive to give your photos away for free, in reality this can be more accurately thought of as free advertising as opposed to charity. The truth of the matter is that if potential customers don't have the money for a stock photo, odds are they are going to end up with the photo they need one way or another. Instead of getting taken advantage of, posting photos in the free section allows potential customers to see your work now, so that they remember it when they are ready to actually spend money on stock photos at a point in the future. Additionally, it will ensure that your name gets out there as well, and the easier your name is to find online, the easier it will be for you to get paid for your photos.

Chapter 8:
Rental Property
as a Passive Income Stream

Depending on the overall amount of time and effort you spend looking, as well as your credit score and how just plain lucky you are, there will always be passive income real estate investment opportunities that require very little cash up front. Unfortunately, these types of deals are going to be the exception to the rule, however, which means that you are generally going to need a greater amount of starter investment capital to take advantage of the following suggestions. With that being said, however, it is important to keep in mind that they are all virtually guaranteed to make a reliable return on your investment when executed properly.

Assuming you go into this passive income opportunity with the goal of utilizing a property management company to handle the active aspect of rental property ownership, owning rental properties can be an extremely passive way to earn a reliable amount of income in both the relatively short as well as the long term. However, you will also need to determine what types of property the property management companies in the area you are interested in purchasing property in will work with as most property management companies will not work with individuals who only have a single, single family home for rent. In general, your best bet in these types of scenarios is to go for either a duplex or a small apartment complex to start, if not a single condominium and expanding from there.

Condominiums are a great choice for a first passive income rental property for several reasons. First, you know there will always be someone on site and you don't even need to worry about paying additional fees for a property manager. Additionally, the types of renters that are looking for condos are typically upwardly mobile professionals which means you will rarely need to worry about payments being spotty or being made late. On the other hand, a duplex requires less work than an apartment complex, but more than a condo and it will be important to screen potential renters thoroughly to ensure you don't get stuck paying for the property while dealing with getting someone evicted. Finally, a small apartment complex is nice because you don't need to worry about paying your bills as long as a simple majority of tenants can pay their rent on time. As an added bonus, if you can find a reliable person to be your on premises representation then you might not even need to hire a property management company.

How to tell a good rental property from a bad one: When it comes to choosing the right property, the first thing you are going to want to do is start by looking at the neighborhood the property you are considering is located in, both during the day as well as at night. You will also want to find other renters in the area and ask or their opinion on the neighborhood as a whole. It is important you ask renters these questions as they are less likely to make things sound better than they are because they almost always have little to no stake in the neighborhood as a whole.

You will also want to ensure that the property tax in the area that you are looking in is less than or equal to the average for the broader area. Property tax rates can vary dramatically from neighborhood to neighborhood and failing to take these sorts of things into account has the potential to seriously affect your profit margins if you are unlucky. Additionally, you are going to want to consider properties that require as little upfront work as possible, because the longer a property stays empty, the longer your money is going to be tied up in the investment and not actively working for you.

When looking for a property it is also important to always go into it with a target renter in mind. For a passive income stream you are going to typically want to stick with families, simply because moving four or more people is much more difficult than just one or two. This means you are going to want to consider the amenities in the area, including things such as schools or parks. Don't forget to scope out the local job market as well, both in terms of its strength right now, but also for major developments that could be coming up in the relatively near future. Not only can this prevent you from buying into an area right before an economic downturn, if you listen to the right rumor, you can get into a new area before positive construction starts that will raise the value of the whole area.

Charge the right amount for rent: Once you find a property that appears as though it meets your needs, the next thing you are going to want to do is to run the potential numbers to ensure it is actually going to be worth it for you to move forward. This means you are going to want to look into the current rental prices for other, similar properties in the area so you can get a basic idea of what's reasonable before factoring in the things that make the property you are looking into unique and adjusting accordingly. Once you have a number in mind, all you need to do is add up the cost that you will pay for insurance, loan payment, property management fees and taxes and subtract that result from the likely rent amount.

Whatever is leftover is what you as the property owner are going to be entitled to, if it seems like a reasonable number to you then you can go ahead with the property. You will also need to factor in another 10 percent of the total costs to account for any vacancies or missed payments that you can expect to experience now and then. Additionally, you can plan on the property appreciating 3 percent each year, which should be enough to pay for some of the existing fees.

Have a clear plan in mind to start: Before you ever start looking at houses, you are going to want to have a clear idea of what you can expect in terms of bank loans, cash on hand, owner-financing and hard money loans. Going in with a clear number will help you to limit your search to reasonable levels while also keeping you in the realm of reality when it comes to finding the perfect investment property for you. Additionally, this will help you to ensure that when it comes time to actually negotiate a deal, you know what your ideal number is, what the worst number you can accept is and when you absolutely, positively have to walk away. Once you know these numbers, don't let your emotions get in the way in the moment, stick with them strictly and you will never be disappointed in the results.

Chapter 9:
Invest in REITs

REITs, otherwise known by their full name, real estate investment trusts, are to real estate what stocks are to business ownership. In fact, they were created expressly to give those who might never otherwise be able to afford it, a way to experience the benefits of major property ownership. In this instance, you choose a brokerage firm or a Roth IRA to invest your money for you, and then they do so in the form of purchasing the equivalent of shares in various types of real estate. In return, you will receive dividend payments at scheduled periods on par with the portion of the real estate in question that you already own.

The biggest downside of this type of passive income is that if you don't put it into a retirement account the profits you make will be taxed, even though you already paid taxes on the money when it was originally earned. There is less overall risk, though, and you only have to put down as much money as you are comfortable with, which means you will get all the benefits of property ownership without having to take out a loan. Additionally, REIT share owners are able to see the relative prices that their shares are worth at any time which means that if the price ever gets too good to resist they can simply cash out without worrying about going through the rigmarole of a traditional real estate transaction.

However, for those who are looking for a passive income stream to supplement their retirement income, then there is really very little downside. Additional benefits include guaranteed professional management, and professional investors so you always know that your investment funds are being handled properly. The most important thing you have to do throughout the entire process is choose the right type of REIT for you.

Residential REIT: The most common type of REIT that many passive income investors start off with is a residential REIT which means that it typically works with property in the scope of things like large apartment buildings or condominium communities. You will be able to tell when this type of REIT is a good investment if the amount of demand for this type of housing currently exceeds the demand in the area where the REIT's holdings are located. On the other hand, if you find out that the area the holdings are located in is currently in the midst of a boom construction market then you might want to hold off until things turn in your favor.

Retail REITs: Retail REITs are typically further specialized into either REITs based around owning shopping centers or REITs based around owning shopping malls. You can determine how successful these REITs are currently by first visiting their local holdings to see what state they are currently in. Additionally, you will want to determine what types of plans for relevant construction are currently ongoing in the area, which should be easy to do because these types of projects often aren't undertaken without extensive preplanning beforehand.

Industrial or Office REITs: These REITs are often grouped together because they are both generally subject to leases that last much longer than other types of REITs. This means that determining whether or not either is going to be popular at a given time is all about figuring out how full the properties in question are currently and when the current tenants moved in. Once you know when a tenant moved in, you can then easily determine if the rent they are paying is on par with, above or below, the current standard for similar space by determining what the market was like when they signed their lease. If it was a buyers' market then the rent is likely going to be low, if it was a seller's market then the prices are likely going to be higher.

Health care REITs: One of the most resilient types of REITs, health care REITs rarely experience periods of decline because they focus on hospitals and various hospital related buildings. New hospitals and hospital related buildings are rarely built, and when they are there is typically plenty of planning which means it is generally quite easy to see if a given health care REIT is going to be profitable or not over a specific period of time. Additionally, you are going to want to determine the current federal reimbursement amount for health care spending, if it is increasing then the REIT will likely make money, if it is decreasing then you may want to hold off and see how things shake out.

Storage: When it comes to jumping on the REIT bandwagon, there is no cheaper way to do so than via an REIT that focuses on storage units. Storage unit use has been rising steadily in the United States for the past 20 years and this type of REIT has proven itself to be reliable and quite resistant to downturns as well. As long as there are not too many competing services in a given area, this type of REIT is almost always going to generate slow and steady profits.

Resorts and hotels: At the other end of the spectrum from storage REITs, REITs that focus on resorts and hotels can generate major profits, but they are much more dependent on a strong economy to do so. The first thing that many people cut during a recession is recessionary travel spending which means that these types of REITs are likely going to do very poorly if the economy as a whole is weaker than it is strong. If you are confident in the health of the economy for a relatively prolonged period of time, then there are few better ways, and more profitable, ways of putting your money where your mouth is assuming things go according to plan.

Chapter 10:
Wholesaling Properties

If you are interested in working with real estate on a more personal level, but you don't want to worry about things like improving a property or interacting with it in any way, then wholesaling properties way be the type of real estate passive income investment that you have been waiting for. Essentially, what you are doing when you are wholesaling properties is finding properties with potential for a quality price, getting them under contract and then sharing your find with another investor who then purchases the property from you for slightly more than what you paid for it.

Before you get started, however, it is important to keep in mind that every state has different standards regarding what real estate wholesaling is, and who can do it. Some states consider a real estate wholesaler to be a broker between a buyer and seller and a further subsection then require that all brokers be licensed real estate agents. Other states don't have wholesale laws related to brokering but still require a real estate license to do it, while still others don't have anything on the books about the process at all. Essentially, what all this means for you is that before you get started following the steps below, you are going to want to check with a real estate lawyer in your area to see exactly what is required of you.

If the area that you are currently living in prevents unlicensed individuals from wholesaling a property you will then have two options. First, you can put your passive income stream on hold while you go about becoming an officially licensed real estate, or, you can generally get around the real estate license requirement by doing what is known as a double close instead of simply selling the contract outright. To do so, you start by explaining to the original seller and the ultimate buyer what your plan is to ensure that the seller agrees to move forward with the sale without receiving a down payment. Then, after the deal has officially closed, you then sell the property to the ultimate buyer so your sales contract closes after the purchase agreement has already closed. The second transaction then pays for the original sale and everyone can walk away happy.

1. *Know the numbers:* When it comes to using property wholesaling as a passive income stream, the time you spend on it will be related to first, finding the perfect properties, and second, marketing them to interested buyers. First and foremost, when it comes to finding properties that are worthwhile, you are going to want to follow the same general process as if you were looking for a property to purchase for rental opportunities, though you will need to be a bit choosier in order to find property you can make a profit off of. To do so, you are going to want to start by determining the after repair value (ARV) of any property that you are considering. As the name implies, the after repair value is what you estimate the property is going to be worth once everything is said and done. With this number in mind you can then determine what you can afford to offer the seller while still making a profit and presenting ultimate potential buyers with a deal that they can still make a profit on as well.

2. *Find the right properties:* When it comes to finding the right properties that you and the ultimate buyer can both make a profit on, you are going to need to use different methods than when looking for other types of properties. A good place to start is with a real estate agent who specializes in bank foreclosures, while this will further cut into your profits, it will also

dramatically reduce the amount of time you need to spend doing your own research. Another great way to cut down on your research time is to look online and find a local business that will sell you a list of individuals with serious outstanding debts. You can then use this information to find out which of these individuals own property and seek them out directly.

Along these same lines you can often visit your county assessor's office and find records of property that is in the starter phase of the foreclosure process. Either way, you are getting to individuals who have not yet spoken to a realtor and who are clearly in a financial predicament, a potent combination when it comes to getting a price on a property that you can actually work with.

While it may sound old fashioned, studies show that the best way to reach out to these individuals is with a direct mail campaign. In the letter you send out you are going to want to explain where you came across their information, that you are sorry for their current situation and how you can help them out of their current predicament. The average rate of return on these types of letters is roughly 3 percent. While that might not seem like a lot, 3 houses out of a hundred can easily work out to $20,000 or more, simply for moving some paper around and getting a few signatures.

3. *Find the ultimate buyer:* When it comes to finding a buyer for the properties that you manage to wholesale, instead of casting a broad net online, you are going to want to strive to find someone local for the best results. Your goal should be to build a relationship with a house flipper in your area who either has cash on hand or

access to hard money loans, this way you will get your money right away, as soon as the final sale goes through. What's more, assuming you find the right flipper, they are the only person you ever need to deal with because they will always be ready for a new property by the time you find another deal that will work for you. The best place to find these types of buyers is through a local real estate buyer's club because these individuals will likely have the local connections that you are looking for.

Conclusion

Thank you for making it through to the end of *Passive Income: Definitive Beginner's Guide to Quit Your Day Job Through Multiple Income Streams*, let's hope it was informative and able to provide you with all of the tools you need to achieve your goals both in the near term and for the months and years ahead. Remember, just because you've finished this book doesn't mean there is nothing left to learn on the topic. Becoming an expert at something is a marathon, not a sprint, slow and steady wins the race.

The next step is to stop reading already and to get started deciding what type of passive income stream you are most interested in pursuing on first. Whichever you choose, it is important to ensure you are properly prepared at the start and that you have a timetable properly planned out as well so you know when you are in it for the long haul. Additionally, you will want to have realistic expectations as to what you can hope to see in terms of returns in both the short and the long term. Only by being completely prepared can you hope to see the biggest returns on your investment and you can only be prepared when you know exactly what it is in you are in for. This way you can stick with it and find the success you deserve!

Finally, if you found this book useful in anyway, a review on Amazon is always appreciated!

Good luck!

www.ingramcontent.com/pod-product-compliance
Lightning Source LLC
Chambersburg PA
CBHW071831200526
45169CB00018B/1310